WHERE FOOD COMES FROM

SEEDS TO BREAD

Sarah Ridley

CRABTREE
PUBLISHING COMPANY
WWW.CRABTREEBOOKS.COM

Published in Canada
Crabtree Publishing
616 Welland Avenue
St. Catharines, ON
L2M 5V6

Published in the United States
Crabtree Publishing
PMB 59051
350 Fifth Ave, 59th Floor
New York, NY 10118

Published in 2019 by Crabtree Publishing Company

First Published in Great Britain in 2018 by Wayland
Copyright © Hodder and Stoughton, 2018

Author: Sarah Ridley

Editors: Sarah Peutrill, Petrice Custance

Design: Matt Lilly

Proofreader: Ellen Rodger

Prepress technician: Margaret Amy Salter

Print coordinator: Katharine Berti

Printed in the U.S.A./082018/CG20180601

Photographs

bestpromo/Shutterstock: 3t. bgphoto/istockphoto: 10. Burwell Photography/istockphoto: 17b. Pavel Chagochkin/Shutterstock: 16. dja65/istockphoto: 5l. Clynt Garnham/Alamy: 7. Joe Gough/Shutterstock: 3b. ifong/Shutterstock: 23. Juice Images/Alamy: 15. Lepas/Shutterstock: 11. Max Maier/Shutterstock: 12, 24tr. Maksud/Shutterstock: 6. MarkUK97/Shutterstock: 3c. mkos83/Shutterstock: front cover b, 1b. nfmlk/Shutterstock: 5br. Tyler Olson/Shutterstock: 2, 18. Ortodox/Shutterstock: 8b. oticki/Shutterstock: 9. Petro Pertruskyi/Shutterstock: 8t. photology1971/istockphoto: 19. Angela Rohde/Shutterstock: 21b, 24l. RTImages/Shutterstock: 22. Sensor Spot/istockphoto: 21t. Ariel Skelley/Getty Images: 4. smereka/Shutterstock: 13, 14. Volosina/Shutterstock: front cover t, 1t. wavebreakmedia/istockphoto: 20. xpixel/Shutterstock: 17t.

Library and Archives Canada Cataloguing in Publication

Ridley, Sarah, 1963-, author
    Seeds to bread / Sarah Ridley.

(Where food comes from)
Includes index.
Issued in print and electronic formats.
ISBN 978-0-7787-5128-1 (hardcover).--
ISBN 978-0-7787-5132-8 (softcover).--
ISBN 978-1-4271-2169-1 (HTML)

    1. Bread--Juvenile literature. 2. Wheat--Processing--Juvenile literature.
I. Title.

TX769.R53 2018   j664'.722   C2018-902475-5
                                                   C2018-902476-3

Library of Congress Cataloging-in-Publication Data

CIP available at the Library of Congress

CONTENTS

NAAN

BAGUETTE

SLICES OF TOAST

There are so many kinds of bread to enjoy. Bread is made from wheat.

But where does wheat come from?

WHAT IS WHEAT?

Wheat is a cereal crop grown by farmers in their fields.

WHEAT FACT

Wheat, barley, oats, rye, and rice are all cereal crops grown by farmers to produce food.

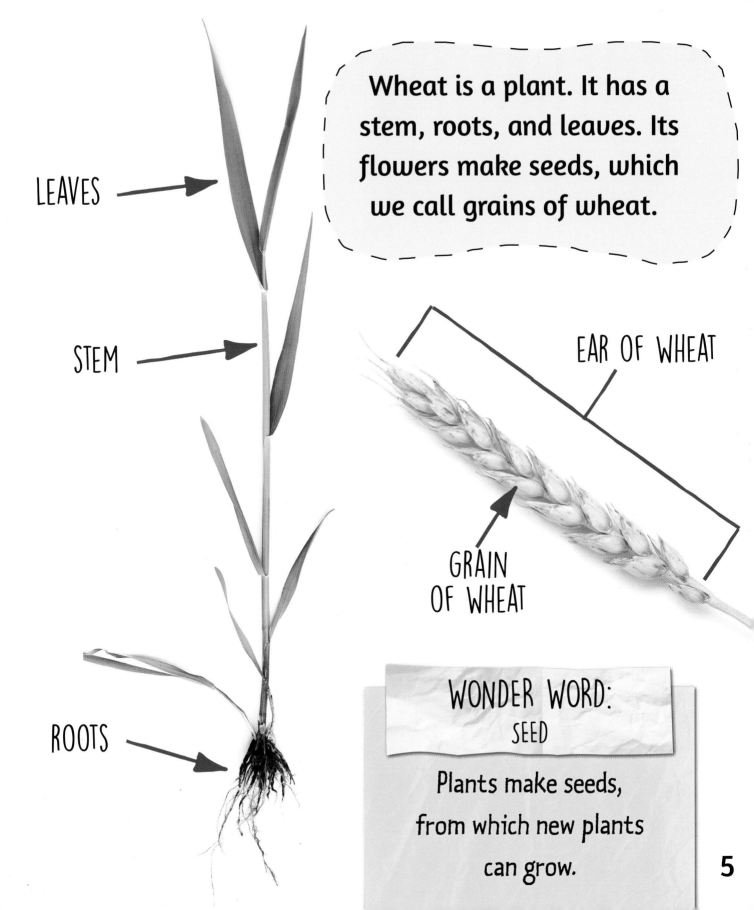

LEAVES

STEM

ROOTS

Wheat is a plant. It has a stem, roots, and leaves. Its flowers make seeds, which we call grains of wheat.

EAR OF WHEAT

GRAIN OF WHEAT

WONDER WORD:
SEED

Plants make seeds, from which new plants can grow.

5

GROWING WHEAT

In late summer or autumn, farmers prepare their fields for planting seeds. Tractors pull plows to turn the soil upside down.

Now it is time to **sow** the wheat seeds using a seed drill. The drill drops seeds into a narrow **trench** and covers them with soil.

Under the ground, each seed swells and develops a shoot and roots. After a few days, the green shoots push through the soil and start growing. They turn into small plants called seedlings.

The seedlings' leaves make food for the plants using air, water, and sunlight. Farmers sometimes spray **fertilizer** to give extra food to the wheat, or **pesticide** to kill insects or diseases.

WHEAT FACT

The wheat grows slowly over winter but faster in spring, due to warmer weather and longer days.

At the end of spring, ears of wheat form at the top of the stems. Each ear of wheat grows tiny flowers that make pollen. The wind blows pollen from one plant to another. This is called **pollination**.

WHEAT FLOWERS

WONDER WORD:
POLLEN

Pollen is a fine powder that causes plants to form seeds.

Pollination allows the flowers to make seeds called grains. All summer, the grains swell in the warm sunshine.

HARVESTING WHEAT

By the end of summer, the wheat fields have changed color, from green to gold. The wheat ears bend from the weight of the **ripe** grains.

On hot dry days, farmers drive **combines** to their fields to **harvest** their crops. The combines cut the wheat and collect the grain.

Inside the combine, a machine separates the grains from the ears of wheat. When the combine's tank is full, the driver pushes a button to empty the grain into a **trailer**.

The tractor and trailer return to the farmyard to unload the wheat. It is dried and stored until the farmer sells the wheat to a flour mill.

WHEAT FACT

Some of the wheat grown by farmers is used to make bread flour. The rest is made into other types of flour, breakfast cereals, pasta, or animal feed.

WHEAT BECOMES FLOUR

At the flour mill, the wheat grains are cleaned before they pass through rollers. The rollers split the grains into three parts—**bran, wheat germ,** and white flour.

WHEAT FACT

Wheat can be made into many types of flour, including all-purpose flour, bread flour, self-rising flour, pastry flour, and whole-wheat flour.

Giant **sieves** remove the bran and the wheat germ to make white flour.

WHITE FLOUR

WHOLE GRAINS

Bran and wheat germ are left in the flour to make whole-wheat flour.

WHOLE—WHEAT FLOUR

The flour is poured into bags and sold to bakeries, food factories, and grocery stores.

FLOUR BECOMES BREAD

At this bakery they are starting to make bread. The baker empties a bag of flour into a machine along with some water.

WHEAT FACT

It takes about 350 ears of wheat to make enough flour for one loaf of bread.

Next, the baker adds small amounts of yeast, salt, and fat. The machine mixes it all together to form stretchy dough. The dough is left to rise.

WONDER WORD:
YEAST

Yeast is a tiny living organism. It feeds on sugars in the dough and releases bubbles of gas that make the dough rise.

The bakers knead and shape the dough into loaves of bread.

The baker slides the loaves into a hot oven.

When the loaves of bread are cooked and cool, they are shipped to bakeries and grocery stores.

HEALTHY BREAD

Bread is an important food that gives us energy to work and play. It also contains important **nutrients** and fiber that help the body stay healthy.

WONDER WORD:
FIBER

Fiber helps your body to **digest** food. Whole-wheat bread contains more fiber, vitamins, and minerals than white bread.

Look at the photo below. Can you spot the food group that has bread in it?

For a healthy and balanced diet, eat more foods from the larger groups and less foods from the smaller groups.

GLOSSARY

bran The skin of the wheat grain

combine A machine that harvests grain

digest To break down food in the body

fertilizer A substance that provides nutrients to soil

harvest To gather a crop

mill A building with machinery to grind grain into flour

nutrients Natural substances found in foods that the body needs to function and stay healthy

pesticide Chemicals used to destroy insects or pests

pollination The spreading of pollen from one flower to another, allowing plants to make fruit and seeds

ripe Ready to harvest

sieve A mesh device that flour is strained through

sow To plant or scatter seeds

trailer A wagon on wheels used to transport goods

trench A long, narrow hole in the soil

wheat germ The middle part of the wheat grain, containing vitamins

INDEX